LLC S-Corp for Beginners 2025

Mastering Limited Liability Company Formation, Management, S-Corp Tax Strategies, Compliance and Day-to-Day Operations

Copyright.

Copyright © MJ Young, 2024

All rights reserved. No part of this publication may be reproduced, distributed, or transmitted in any form or by any means, including photocopying, recording, or other electronic or mechanical methods, without the prior written permission of the publisher, except in the case of brief quotations embodied in critical reviews and certain other noncommercial uses permitted by copyright law.

Introduction

Starting and managing a business is an exciting journey filled with both opportunity and challenge.

Whether you're an entrepreneur launching your first venture, a small business owner looking to optimize your tax strategy, or someone seeking greater protection for your personal assets, understanding the right business structure is crucial for long-term success.

One of the most popular business structures among small business owners is the LLC (Limited Liability Company) taxed as an S-Corp (S Corporation). But with popularity comes complexity.

Choosing to operate as an LLC with S-Corp tax status can offer significant advantages—ranging from asset protection and tax savings to flexibility in management—but only if you understand how to properly form, manage, and maintain this entity.

This book is designed to simplify that process for you.

Why This Book?

LLC S-Corp for Beginners 2025 is your practical guide to mastering the ins and outs of setting up, managing, and growing an LLC S-Corp.

We'll walk you through everything from the initial steps of formation, such as choosing the right name and filing the necessary paperwork, to understanding advanced tax strategies that can save you thousands of dollars.

We'll also dive into the ongoing responsibilities of running an LLC S-Corp, from maintaining compliance with state laws to keeping up with federal tax filings.

You'll discover how to make informed decisions that will protect your business, maximize profitability, and allow you to focus on growth rather than getting bogged down in legal and financial details.

Who Is This Book For?

This book is tailored for beginners—those with little to no experience with LLCs or S-Corps. If you've ever felt overwhelmed by the legal jargon, tax regulations, or compliance requirements, you're not alone.

Whether you're a solo entrepreneur, a small business owner, or someone curious about LLC S-Corps, this guide will give you the knowledge and confidence to move forward with ease.

What You'll Learn

In this book, we will cover:

- The benefits of forming an LLC with S-Corp tax status
- Step-by-step instructions for setting up your LLC S-Corp
- Essential tax strategies to reduce your tax burden
- Ongoing compliance and management best practices
- Day-to-day operations, hiring, and managing finances
- Advanced topics such as business growth, risk management, and succession planning

How to Use This Book

Whether you're reading this book cover to cover or jumping to specific sections as needed, LLC S-Corp for Beginners 2025 is designed to serve as both a learning tool and a reference guide.

Each chapter builds upon the last, guiding you through the process from initial formation to more advanced operations.

In addition to the core concepts, we'll provide real-world examples, practical tips, and sample forms to make your journey as smooth as possible.

Your Business, Your Future

Forming an LLC S-Corp is more than just a legal or tax decision—it's a strategic choice that can safeguard your assets, reduce your tax burden, and enhance your business's credibility. With this book, you'll gain the knowledge and tools you need to make the right decisions for your future and set your business on the path to success.

Let's get started on the journey to mastering your LLC S-Corp and taking control of your business future!

Table of Contents

Copyright.
Introduction
Table of Contents
Part 1: Introduction to LLC S-Corps
Chapter 1: Benefits of Forming an LLC S-Corp
Chapter 2: Understanding LLCs and S-Corps
    Definition and Purpose
    Key Characteristics
    Comparison to Other Business Structures
Chapter 3: Eligibility and Restrictions
    Who Can Form an LLC S-Corp?
    Restrictions on Ownership and Management
Part 2: Formation and Setup
Chapter 4: Choosing a Business Name and Registering Your LLC
    Name Selection and Availability
    Filing Articles of Organization
    Obtaining an EIN
Chapter 6: Obtaining Licenses and Permits
    Business Licenses
    Professional Licenses
    Local Permits
Chapter 7: Setting Up Accounting and Bookkeeping Systems
    Accounting Methods
    Bookkeeping Best Practices
    Financial Statement Preparation
Part 3: S-Corp Taxation
Chapter 8: Understanding S-Corp Taxation
    Pass-Through Taxation
    Tax Benefits
    Tax Obligations
Chapter 9: S-Corp Tax Filing Requirements
    Form 1120S
    Schedule K-1
    Other Tax Forms
Chapter 10: Tax Strategies for S-Corps
    Minimizing Self-Employment Tax
    Maximizing Deductions

    Avoiding Common Tax Pitfalls
Part 4: Compliance and Maintenance
    Chapter 11: Maintaining S-Corp Status
    Annual Reporting Requirements
    Compliance with Tax Laws
    Record-Keeping Best Practices
Chapter 12: Handling Changes in Ownership and Management
    Adding or Removing Owners
    Changing Management Structure
    Amending the Operating Agreement
Chapter 13: Dissolving an LLC S-Corp
    Reasons for Dissolution
    Step-by-Step Dissolution Process
    Post-Dissolution Obligations
Part 5: Day-to-Day Operations
Chapter 14: Managing Finances and Cash Flow
    Budgeting and Forecasting
    Managing Accounts Receivable and Payable
    Cash Flow Management Strategies
Chapter 15: Hiring and Managing Employees
    Recruitment and Hiring
    Employee Benefits and Compensation
    Termination and Separation
Chapter 16: Maintaining Business Records and Compliance
    Record-Keeping Requirements
    Document Retention Policies
    Compliance with Regulatory Requirements
Part 6: Advanced Topics and Best Practices
Chapter 17: Advanced Tax Strategies
    Section 179 Deductions
    Bonus Depreciation
    Other Advanced Tax Strategies
Chapter 18: Business Growth and Expansion
    Strategies for Growth
    Managing Expansion
    Avoiding Common Pitfalls
Chapter 19: Best Practices for LLC S-Corps
    Governance and Decision-Making
    Risk Management
    Succession Planning
Conclusion

Chapter 20: Putting it All Together
Recap of Key Concepts
    Next Steps for LLC S-Corp Owners
    Resources for Further Learning

Part 1: Introduction to LLC S-Corps

Chapter 1: Benefits of Forming an LLC S-Corp

When starting a business, one of the first decisions you'll make is choosing the right legal structure.

An LLC (Limited Liability Company) taxed as an S-Corp (S Corporation) is a popular option because it offers several key benefits. Let's break them down in simple terms:

Asset Protection

As a business owner, your personal savings, home, and other assets are valuable. One of the main reasons people choose to form an LLC is to protect these personal assets.

If your business runs into legal trouble or has debt, forming an LLC helps keep your personal finances separate from your business finances.

This means that, in most cases, your personal assets won't be at risk if your business faces lawsuits or financial issues. The LLC "limits" your personal liability, which is one of its biggest advantages.

Tax Benefits

When you choose S-Corp tax status for your LLC, you can take advantage of certain tax benefits. Here's the basic idea: usually, business owners have to pay self-employment taxes on their entire income.

But with an S-Corp, you can reduce how much of your income is taxed this way by paying yourself a "reasonable salary" and taking the rest as distributions (a kind of business profit).

The result? You could pay less in taxes overall.

Flexibility in Ownership and Management

One of the great things about an LLC is how flexible it is. Unlike other business types that have strict rules about how many owners you can have or who can manage the company, an LLC gives you options.

You can have just one owner or multiple owners, and you can decide who will be responsible for running the business.

When you add S-Corp tax status, it keeps this flexibility while also giving you tax advantages. It's a win-win for many business owners.

Enhanced Credibility

An LLC S-Corp can make your business look more professional and trustworthy. Customers, suppliers, and even lenders often see an LLC as more established and credible than a sole proprietorship or partnership.

This can open doors for business opportunities and make it easier to get contracts, loans, or customers.

Conclusion

Choosing to form an LLC with S-Corp tax status is an important step in protecting your personal assets, reducing taxes, and positioning your business for success.

Whether you're just starting out or looking to improve your existing business structure, the benefits of an LLC S-Corp offer flexibility, credibility, and peace of mind.

In the next chapter, we'll dive deeper into understanding what LLCs and S-Corps are and how they compare to other business structures, helping you make a more informed decision for your business.

Chapter 2: Understanding LLCs and S-Corps

To make the best decision for your business, it's crucial to understand what LLCs and S-Corps are and how they function.

This chapter will break down the definitions, key characteristics, and how these business structures compare to others.

Definition and Purpose

LLC (Limited Liability Company)

An LLC is a legal structure designed to protect the personal assets of its owners, called "members."

Think of it as creating a protective barrier between your personal finances and your business. If your business gets sued or accumulates debt, your personal bank account, house, or car are typically safe from being taken to cover those costs.

The purpose of an LLC is to offer flexibility in managing and running the business while offering personal liability protection.

S-Corp (S Corporation)

An S-Corp isn't actually a type of business entity like an LLC. Instead, it's a special tax classification that businesses (like LLCs or corporations) can choose.

The purpose of an S-Corp status is to help owners save money on taxes, particularly by reducing the amount of self-employment taxes you have to pay.

When you elect to be taxed as an S-Corp, you split your income into two parts: a salary (which is taxed like regular wages) and distributions (which are taxed at a lower rate). This can lead to significant tax savings.

Key Characteristics

LLC Characteristics

Liability Protection: As mentioned, one of the biggest benefits of an LLC is that it shields your personal assets from business liabilities.

Flexible Management: LLCs can be managed by the owners themselves (member-managed) or by someone they appoint (manager-managed).

Pass-through Taxation: LLCs don't pay corporate taxes. Instead, profits and losses are "passed through" to the owners, who report them on their personal tax returns.

Fewer Formalities: Unlike corporations, LLCs generally have fewer requirements when it comes to formal meetings or maintaining strict records.

S-Corp Characteristics

Tax Savings: The primary reason people elect S-Corp status is to reduce self-employment taxes by splitting income between salary and distributions.

Ownership Limits: S-Corps have some restrictions, such as allowing a maximum of 100 shareholders, and all shareholders must be U.S. citizens or residents.

Pass-through Taxation: Like LLCs, S-Corps also benefit from pass-through taxation, meaning the corporation itself doesn't pay income taxes, and profits are reported on individual returns.

More Formal Requirements: S-Corps require more formalities, such as issuing stock, holding regular meetings, and maintaining records.

Comparison to Other Business Structures

LLC vs. Sole Proprietorship

A sole proprietorship is the simplest form of business. You and the business are legally the same, meaning there's no separation between your personal and business assets. An LLC, by contrast, protects your personal assets from business liabilities.

Tax-wise, both are treated similarly in that income flows through to your personal taxes, but LLCs offer more protection and flexibility in management.

S-Corp vs. C-Corp

A C-Corp is a standard corporation that pays taxes on its profits, and then shareholders are taxed again on any dividends they receive (this is known as double taxation).

An S-Corp avoids this double taxation because profits flow directly to the owners' personal tax returns.

However, C-Corps have no restrictions on ownership or how many shareholders they can have, while S-Corps have strict rules on these aspects.

LLC S-Corp vs. Partnership

A partnership involves two or more individuals sharing the ownership of a business. Partnerships have no liability protection, meaning partners are personally responsible for business debts.

In contrast, an LLC S-Corp gives personal liability protection, and its tax structure can be more advantageous depending on the income level.

Conclusion

Understanding the differences between LLCs and S-Corps is essential for choosing the right structure for your business.

An LLC offers liability protection and management flexibility, while an S-Corp provides tax advantages that can help you keep more of your earnings.

By knowing the characteristics and comparing them with other business structures, you can determine whether forming an LLC with S-Corp status fits your business goals.

In the next chapter, we'll discuss who is eligible to form an LLC S-Corp and the restrictions you need to be aware of.

Chapter 3: Eligibility and Restrictions

Before jumping into the process of forming an LLC S-Corp, it's essential to understand whether you qualify and what restrictions might apply.

Not every business is eligible for S-Corp status, and certain rules about ownership and management need to be followed.

This chapter will guide you through who can form an LLC S-Corp and the limitations you should keep in mind.

Who Can Form an LLC S-Corp?

LLCs in General

Anyone who wants to start a business can form an LLC in the United States.

There are no specific restrictions based on nationality, type of business, or number of owners (called members). LLCs can be formed by individuals, multiple partners, or even other companies.

The flexibility in ownership and structure is one of the reasons LLCs are so popular among small businesses and entrepreneurs.

S-Corp Eligibility

When it comes to electing S-Corp status for your LLC, there are specific requirements set by the IRS.

Here's a breakdown of the main criteria:

U.S. Citizenship or Residency: All shareholders (or owners, in the case of an LLC) must be U.S. citizens or legal residents. This means non-resident aliens are not allowed to be part of an LLC that elects S-Corp status.

Limited Number of Owners: An LLC electing S-Corp status can have no more than 100 owners (called shareholders in corporations or members in LLCs). For most small businesses, this won't be an issue, but it's important to know this limit.

Eligible Entities: Only certain types of businesses can qualify for S-Corp status. Specifically, LLCs and corporations are eligible, but partnerships, certain banks, and insurance companies are not allowed to elect S-Corp taxation.

Restrictions on Ownership and Management

Ownership Restrictions

While LLCs are very flexible in terms of who can own the company, S-Corp status places some restrictions on ownership. Let's explore these restrictions:

No Non-Resident Owners: As mentioned earlier, only U.S. citizens or residents can be members of an LLC S-Corp.

If your business plans to bring in foreign investors or owners, electing S-Corp status may not be the right choice.

Single Class of Stock: If your LLC chooses S-Corp taxation, you can only issue one class of ownership. In simpler terms, this means that all owners (or members) must have the same rights when it comes to distributions and voting power.

In a standard corporation, companies can issue multiple classes of stock with different voting rights, but this is not allowed for an S-Corp.

Management Restrictions

LLCs are generally flexible when it comes to management structures. You can choose whether the company is managed by the owners (members) or by appointed managers.

However, if your LLC has elected S-Corp status, you'll need to follow specific rules for handling the company's financials and compensation:

Reasonable Salary Requirement: One key rule for S-Corp taxation is that if you are an owner-employee (meaning you actively work in the business), you must pay yourself a "reasonable salary."

This salary will be subject to payroll taxes. The IRS requires this to prevent people from paying themselves very low salaries and taking the majority of income as distributions (which are taxed at a lower rate).

Figuring out what a reasonable salary is will depend on your industry and the work you do.

Corporate Formalities: Unlike a standard LLC, which has few formal requirements, an LLC taxed as an S-Corp must follow certain corporate formalities, like holding annual meetings, keeping detailed minutes, and maintaining accurate financial records.

These steps help the IRS ensure that your business is functioning like a legitimate corporation rather than just a way to save on taxes.

Conclusion

Not every business is eligible to form an LLC S-Corp, and there are important restrictions on ownership and management that need to be followed.

While LLCs offer a lot of flexibility in ownership, electing S-Corp status brings specific rules, like the requirement that all owners be U.S. citizens or residents and that there be only one class of ownership.

Understanding these eligibility criteria and restrictions is essential before moving forward.

In the next chapter, we'll cover the steps involved in choosing a business name and registering your LLC, setting you on the path to forming your company.

Part 2: Formation and Setup

Chapter 4: Choosing a Business Name and Registering Your LLC

One of the first and most exciting steps in forming your LLC is choosing a business name and officially registering your company with your state.

Your business name represents your brand, so it's important to select one that reflects your business values while also meeting legal requirements.

Once you've settled on a name, you'll need to file your Articles of Organization and obtain an Employer Identification Number (EIN) to officially establish your business.

Name Selection and Availability

Choosing the Right Name

Your business name is often the first impression you make on customers, so it's important to choose a name that's memorable, unique, and reflective of your business's mission or services.

When brainstorming, consider the following:

Reflect Your Brand: Your business name should give people an idea of what your company does. Whether you're a consulting firm, a food service provider, or a tech startup, your name should align with your industry.

Keep It Simple: A name that's easy to pronounce, spell, and remember is key to making it stick in people's minds. Avoid overly complicated or long names, and check if a related domain name is available if you plan on having an online presence.

Future-Proof: Consider how your business might evolve over time. You may not want to choose a name that's too specific, which could limit your company's growth in the future.

Checking Name Availability

Once you've picked a few potential names, you'll need to verify that your name isn't already in use or trademarked.

Each state has its own requirements, but here are the general steps:

State Name Search: You can check the availability of your business name by conducting a search through your state's business registry. Many states offer this service online through their Secretary of State website.

Trademark Search: It's also important to ensure that your business name isn't trademarked by someone else, as this could lead to legal issues.

You can search the U.S. Patent and Trademark Office (USPTO) website to make sure your name isn't already registered.

Domain Name Check: If you plan on having a website, it's smart to check if your chosen business name is available as a domain name (e.g., .com, .net). This will help create a cohesive brand online.

Filing Articles of Organization

What are Articles of Organization?

The Articles of Organization is a legal document you file with the state to formally establish your LLC.

This document outlines the essential information about your business, including its name, address, and the names of its members (owners).

The process for filing Articles of Organization varies slightly by state, but most states have an online submission process that is easy to navigate.

Key Informations Included

Business Name: The name you chose and confirmed is available.

Business Address: You'll need to provide the physical location of your business. This could be your home address if you're running a home-based business.

Registered Agent: The registered agent is a person or entity that receives official legal documents on behalf of your business. This can be you, another member, or a third-party service.

Management Structure: You'll indicate whether your LLC is member-managed (where all members share responsibility) or manager-managed (where designated managers handle daily operations).

Filing Process

Once you have all the necessary information, you can file your Articles of Organization with your state's business authority, typically the Secretary of State's office.

There is usually a filing fee involved, which varies depending on the state. The approval process can take anywhere from a few days to a few weeks, depending on your state's processing times.

Obtaining an EIN

What is an EIN?

An Employer Identification Number (EIN), sometimes referred to as a Federal Tax Identification Number, is a unique number assigned to your business by the IRS.

It's like a Social Security number for your company and is required for tax purposes, even if you don't have employees. It is also necessary for opening a business bank account and applying for certain licenses.

Why You Need an EIN

Tax Filings: You'll need an EIN to file federal and state taxes.

Hiring Employees: If you plan to hire employees, an EIN is required for payroll and tax reporting purposes.

Opening Business Bank Accounts: Most banks require an EIN to open a business bank account.

Business Licenses: Some licenses and permits require an EIN, even if you don't have employees.

How to Get an EIN

Obtaining an EIN is a simple process and can be done directly through the IRS website. The online application is free and typically only takes a few minutes to complete.

You can also apply by fax or mail, but online is by far the quickest method. Once your application is approved, you'll receive your EIN immediately.

Conclusion

Choosing a business name, filing your Articles of Organization, and obtaining an EIN are foundational steps in forming your LLC.

These actions formalize your business, ensuring it's legally recognized and ready to operate. With your business name secured and your LLC officially registered, you're now ready to move forward with other important tasks, such as drafting an operating agreement.

In the next chapter, we'll dive into the importance of having a solid operating agreement in place to define how your LLC will run.

Chapter 6: Obtaining Licenses and Permits

After forming your LLC, one of the critical steps to ensure your business operates legally is obtaining the necessary licenses and permits.

This process varies depending on your industry, location, and the specific type of business you're running. Licenses and permits not only make your business compliant with government regulations, but they also provide legitimacy and build customer trust.

In this chapter, we will walk you through the different types of licenses and permits you may need and how to go about acquiring them.

Business Licenses

What Is a Business License?

A business license is a document issued by a local, state, or federal government that grants you permission to operate your business.

Most businesses, regardless of their industry, are required to obtain some type of business license. It acts as a government stamp of approval, showing that your business complies with local regulations.

Types of Business Licenses

General Business License: Almost every business, whether it's a brick-and-mortar store, online retailer, or home-based service, needs a general business license.

This is usually issued by your local city or county office and is required to legally operate in that area.

Home-Based Business License: If you're running a business from home, you may need a home-based business license.

Some cities have zoning laws that regulate home businesses, and a license ensures that your operations won't interfere with your neighborhood.

Sales Tax Permit: If your business sells physical products, you'll likely need a sales tax permit (also known as a seller's permit).

This allows you to collect sales tax from customers and remit it to the state.

How to Obtain a Business License

Step 1: Research the specific licenses required by your local city or county. Start by visiting the website of your local government or calling their business licensing office.

Step 2: Apply for the license either online or in person. You'll typically need to provide information about your LLC, such as your business name, address, and Employer Identification Number (EIN).

Step 3: Pay the required fee. Licensing fees vary depending on the location and type of business, but most general business licenses cost between $50 and $100.

Step 4: Receive your license and display it according to local regulations. Some cities may require you to prominently display your business license in your place of business.

Professional Licenses

What Is a Professional License?

Certain businesses require professional licenses in addition to general business licenses.

These licenses are typically industry-specific and are intended to ensure that practitioners meet certain standards of competency and ethics.

Examples of industries that may require professional licenses include law, medicine, real estate, accounting, and construction.

Who Needs a Professional License?

Health and Medical Fields: If your business operates in health care (such as a medical practice, dentistry, or mental health counseling), you must obtain the appropriate professional licenses.

These are often issued by state boards that oversee health professions.

Financial Services: Accountants, financial advisors, and other professionals in the financial services sector need to be licensed by state boards or agencies like FINRA (Financial Industry Regulatory Authority).

Trades and Contractors: Electricians, plumbers, and general contractors need professional licenses from state or local licensing boards. These trades are regulated to ensure safety and compliance with building codes.

How to Obtain a Professional License

Step 1: Check the licensing requirements for your specific industry by contacting your state's professional licensing board. Each profession has different criteria, such as education, exams, or work experience.

Step 2: Submit the necessary documentation, such as proof of education or certification, and complete any required exams.

Step 3: Pay the applicable fees. Professional licensing fees vary widely depending on the industry and location.

Step 4: Once you receive your professional license, stay on top of renewals and continuing education requirements to maintain it.

Local Permits

What Are Local Permits?

In addition to general business and professional licenses, your LLC may need local permits depending on your business activities.

These permits regulate things like signage, zoning, health, and safety compliance. Failing to obtain the necessary permits can result in fines or even the closure of your business.

Common Local Permits

Zoning Permits: Zoning laws regulate where certain types of businesses can operate within a city or town.

If you're opening a retail store, restaurant, or industrial facility, you may need to get a zoning permit to ensure your business is located in an area where it's allowed to operate.

Health Department Permits: Businesses that sell food or beverages, such as restaurants, cafes, and food trucks, need health permits from the local health department.

These permits are intended to ensure that the business complies with food safety standards.

Building Permits: If you're making any physical modifications to your business premises, such as renovations or adding signage, you may need a building permit to ensure that the work complies with local building codes.

How to Obtain Local Permits

Step 1: Determine which permits are required for your specific business and location. You can usually find this information on your city or county's official website.

Step 2: Submit the necessary applications to the appropriate local agencies. This may include providing detailed information about your business activities, location, and plans for any physical modifications.

Step 3: Pay any required fees. Permit fees vary based on the type of permit and the scope of your business operations.

Step 4: Wait for approval. Some permits, especially zoning or health permits, may require an inspection of your business premises before approval is granted.

Conclusion

Acquiring the necessary licenses and permits is a vital step in setting up and maintaining your LLC.

These documents not only keep you compliant with local, state, and federal regulations but also help establish your business as legitimate and trustworthy in the eyes of customers.

By ensuring you have the right business licenses, professional licenses, and local permits, you're laying a solid foundation for your LLC to operate smoothly and avoid legal headaches down the road.

In the next chapter, we'll dive into the process of setting up your accounting and bookkeeping systems, which is another key component of running a successful business.

Chapter 7: Setting Up Accounting and Bookkeeping Systems

Proper accounting and bookkeeping are the backbone of any successful business. Whether you're just starting out or scaling your LLC S-Corp, it's essential to have systems in place that help you keep track of your finances.

Without clear, organized financial records, you risk making poor business decisions, facing tax penalties, or running into cash flow issues.

In this chapter, we will break down accounting methods, best practices for bookkeeping, and how to prepare financial statements—all without overwhelming jargon.

Accounting Methods

What Are Accounting Methods?

An accounting method is the approach your business takes to record income and expenses.

The two primary methods are cash accounting and accrual accounting.

The method you choose can have significant tax implications and will affect how you track your financial performance.

Cash Accounting

Under this method, income is recorded when it is received, and expenses are recorded when they are paid.

This is a straightforward system and is often preferred by smaller businesses because it's easy to understand and manage.

If a customer pays you in February for a job completed in January, you record the income in February when the money actually hits your account.

Accrual Accounting

In this method, income is recorded when it is earned, and expenses are recorded when they are incurred, regardless of when money actually changes hands.

For example, if you complete a service in January but are not paid until February, the income is still recorded in January.

This method provides a clearer picture of your business's financial health but can be more complex to manage.

Choosing the Right Method

If you're a small business with straightforward transactions, cash accounting might be the best fit because it's simpler.

If your business is growing or you deal with lots of accounts payable/receivable, accrual accounting offers a more accurate financial picture and is preferred by most larger businesses.

Once you decide on a method, stick with it unless you have a compelling reason to switch. Note that once your LLC S-Corp reaches a certain revenue threshold, you may be required to switch to accrual accounting by the IRS.

Bookkeeping Best Practices

What Is Bookkeeping?

Bookkeeping is the daily recording of your financial transactions. It involves tracking all the money coming in and going out of your business.

Good bookkeeping ensures that you always have a clear understanding of your business's financial position and makes tax time much easier.

Best Practices for Bookkeeping

Separate Business and Personal Finances: Always keep your personal and business finances separate. This is critical for legal reasons (especially with an LLC or S-Corp) and simplifies your bookkeeping.

Open a separate business bank account and use it for all business-related transactions.

Automate Where Possible: Use accounting software like QuickBooks, Xero, or FreshBooks to automate your bookkeeping tasks.

These tools can connect to your business bank account, track expenses, generate invoices, and even prepare tax forms. Automation saves time and reduces the risk of errors.

Record Transactions Regularly: Don't wait until the end of the month or quarter to update your books.

Make a habit of recording transactions weekly or even daily to avoid errors and missing information. This also ensures that you have an up-to-date view of your financial situation.

Track Receipts and Invoices: Keep copies of all receipts and invoices. Digital tools like Expensify or Wave can help you scan and store receipts, making it easier to track deductible expenses and ensure you have a record for tax purposes.

Reconcile Accounts Monthly: Reconciling your accounts means comparing your internal financial records with your bank statements to ensure everything matches.

This helps catch mistakes, duplicate transactions, or fraudulent charges early on.

Financial Statement Preparation

What Are Financial Statements?

Financial statements provide a snapshot of your business's financial health. There are three key financial statements every business should prepare regularly:

Income Statement (Profit and Loss Statement):
This statement shows your business's revenues, expenses, and profits over a specific period.

It provides insight into whether your business is making or losing money and highlights key areas of income and spending.

Balance Sheet: The balance sheet outlines your business's assets (what you own), liabilities (what you owe), and equity (your net worth) at a specific point in time.

It helps you understand your business's financial position and is essential when applying for loans or attracting investors.

Cash Flow Statement: This statement shows how cash moves in and out of your business over a period.

It tracks cash inflows from operations, investments, and financing, as well as cash outflows like expenses, debt payments, and dividends.

Good cash flow management is essential for keeping your business running smoothly, even when sales are slow.

How to Prepare Financial Statements

Use Accounting Software: Most accounting software will generate these financial statements for you automatically based on the data you enter.

Work with a Professional: If you're unsure about preparing financial statements yourself, consider working with a bookkeeper or accountant.

They can help ensure accuracy and may offer valuable insights on how to improve your financial health.

Review Statements Regularly: Don't wait until tax season to review your financial statements. Review them quarterly or monthly to spot trends, identify problems, and make informed decisions.

Conclusion

Setting up a solid accounting and bookkeeping system is one of the best investments you can make for your LLC S-Corp.

Whether you choose cash or accrual accounting, following best practices like automating tasks, separating finances, and keeping accurate records will keep your business organized and help you avoid costly mistakes.

Financial statements, prepared regularly, will guide your business decisions and help ensure long-term success.

In the next chapter, we'll explore the ins and outs of S-Corp taxation—an area that can offer substantial benefits if managed correctly.

Part 3: S-Corp Taxation

Chapter 8: Understanding S-Corp Taxation

Understanding the tax implications of your LLC S-Corp is crucial for maximizing your financial benefits and ensuring compliance with tax laws.

This chapter will explain the concept of pass-through taxation, outline the tax benefits associated with S-Corps, and clarify your tax obligations as an S-Corp owner, all in straightforward language.

Pass-Through Taxation

What Is Pass-Through Taxation?

Pass-through taxation is a tax treatment that allows income earned by your LLC S-Corp to be passed directly to its owners (also known as shareholders) without being taxed at the corporate level.

Instead of the business paying taxes on its profits, the income is reported on the owners' personal tax returns.

This method avoids the double taxation that occurs in traditional C-Corporations, where the corporation pays taxes on its earnings, and then shareholders pay taxes again on dividends they receive.

How Does It Work?

Here's a simple breakdown of how pass-through taxation functions for an S-Corp:

Earnings and Losses: The S-Corp earns income or incurs losses throughout the year.

Reporting: At the end of the year, the S-Corp files Form 1120S with the IRS, reporting its total income, deductions, and credits.

Schedule K-1: The S-Corp also issues a Schedule K-1 to each shareholder, detailing their share of the corporation's income, losses, and deductions.

Personal Tax Return: Shareholders report the information from the K-1 on their personal tax returns (Form 1040), paying taxes at their individual income tax rates.

This system provides tax efficiency and simplicity, making it easier for business owners to understand their tax liabilities.

Tax Benefits

What Are the Tax Benefits of an S-Corp?

S-Corps offer several tax advantages that can lead to significant savings for business owners:

Avoiding Double Taxation: As previously mentioned, S-Corps benefit from pass-through taxation, meaning profits are taxed only once at the individual level rather than at both the corporate and individual levels.

Self-Employment Tax Savings: In a traditional LLC, all profits are subject to self-employment tax, which is approximately 15.3%.

However, in an S-Corp, only the salary you pay yourself as an employee is subject to self-employment tax. Any additional profits distributed as dividends are not subject to this tax, which can save you a considerable amount of money.

Flexibility in Distributions: S-Corp shareholders can take distributions (payments) from the company in addition to their salary. Since distributions are not subject to self-employment tax, this can help lower your overall tax burden.

Tax Deductions: S-Corps can deduct certain business expenses, including employee salaries, health insurance premiums, and retirement contributions, which further reduces taxable income.

These benefits make S-Corps an attractive option for many small business owners looking to maximize their tax efficiency.

Tax Obligations

What Are Your Tax Obligations as an S-Corp Owner?

While S-Corps provide various tax benefits, they also come with specific obligations that you must adhere to:

Filing Requirements: S-Corps must file Form 1120S annually with the IRS. This form reports the income, deductions, and credits of the S-Corp for the tax year.

Additionally, S-Corps are required to issue Schedule K-1 to each shareholder by the tax filing deadline.

Reasonable Salary Requirement: If you are actively involved in the business, you must pay yourself a reasonable salary for the work you perform.

The IRS requires that this salary be comparable to what similar businesses would pay for the same services.

Failure to pay yourself a reasonable salary can lead to penalties and reclassification of distributions as wages, resulting in additional taxes owed.

State Taxes: Depending on the state where your LLC S-Corp is registered, you may have to pay state-level taxes, such as franchise taxes or corporate income taxes. Each state has different rules, so it's essential to understand your state's requirements.

Estimated Taxes: As an S-Corp shareholder, you may need to make estimated tax payments throughout the year, especially if you expect to owe more than $1,000 in taxes when you file your return. This helps you avoid penalties for underpayment.

Understanding and fulfilling these obligations is vital to maintaining your S-Corp status and avoiding issues with the IRS.

Conclusion

Navigating the world of S-Corp taxation may seem daunting, but grasping the fundamentals—like pass-through taxation, tax benefits, and your obligations—will empower you to make informed decisions that can enhance your business's financial health.

By taking advantage of the tax efficiencies S-Corps offer, you can retain more of your hard-earned profits while ensuring compliance with tax regulations.

In the next chapter, we'll dive deeper into the specific tax filing requirements for S-Corps, ensuring you're prepared when tax season rolls around.

Chapter 9: S-Corp Tax Filing Requirements

To maintain compliance with IRS regulations and avoid penalties, understanding the tax filing requirements for your LLC S-Corp is essential.

This chapter covers the main forms you'll need to file, including Form 1120S, Schedule K-1, and other important tax forms, in clear and straightforward language.

Form 1120S

What Is Form 1120S?

Form 1120S is the tax return specifically designed for S-Corporations. This form reports the income, deductions, gains, losses, and other tax-related information of your S-Corp for the tax year.

When Is It Due?

You must file Form 1120S annually by the 15th day of the third month following the end of your tax year.

For most S-Corps that follow the calendar year, this means the due date is March 15. If this date falls on a weekend or holiday, the deadline extends to the next business day.

What Information Is Required?

Form 1120S requires various pieces of information, including:

Business Information: This includes your LLC S-Corp's name, address, and Employer Identification Number (EIN).

Income and Deductions: You'll need to report all income earned by the S-Corp and any deductions you plan to claim, such as business expenses.

Balance Sheet: The form also requires a balance sheet that shows your business's assets, liabilities, and equity at the end of the tax year.

Filing Form 1120S accurately and on time is crucial to avoid penalties and ensure compliance with IRS regulations.

Schedule K-1

What Is Schedule K-1?

Schedule K-1 is a crucial tax document issued by your S-Corp to its shareholders. This form reports each shareholder's share of the corporation's income, deductions, and credits for the tax year.

Why Is It Important?

Schedule K-1 is essential for each shareholder to accurately report their share of the S-Corp's income on their personal tax returns.

Since S-Corp profits are passed through to the owners, shareholders must use the information provided on Schedule K-1 to report their income on Form 1040.

When Is It Due?

Schedule K-1 must be issued to shareholders by the due date of Form 1120S, which is typically March 15 for calendar-year S-Corps.

What Information Is Included?

The K-1 includes several key details:

Shareholder Information: This section lists the shareholder's name, address, and identifying information, such as their Social Security number or EIN.

Income Distribution: The K-1 reports the shareholder's proportionate share of the S-Corp's income, losses, and other tax items.

Deductions and Credits: Any deductions or credits that the shareholder is entitled to receive are also included.

Ensuring that Schedule K-1 is accurate and timely will help your shareholders report their income correctly and avoid potential IRS issues.

Other Tax Forms

In addition to Form 1120S and Schedule K-1, your S-Corp may need to file other tax forms, depending on your specific circumstances:

Form 941 (Employer's Quarterly Federal Tax Return): If your S-Corp has employees, you must file Form 941 quarterly to report income taxes, Social Security tax, and Medicare tax withheld from employees' paychecks.

Form 940 (Employer's Annual Federal Unemployment Tax Return): If you have employees, you'll also need to file Form 940 annually to report and pay unemployment taxes.

State Tax Forms: Depending on the state in which your S-Corp operates, you may have additional state tax filing requirements.

Each state has its own forms and regulations, so it's important to consult your state's tax authority.

Form 2553 (Election by a Small Business Corporation): If you haven't already done so, this form must be filed to elect S-Corp status. It's usually filed with your first Form 1120S.

Being aware of these additional tax forms will help you stay compliant with all federal and state tax obligations.

Conclusion

Understanding the filing requirements for your S-Corp is vital to maintaining compliance and optimizing your tax situation.

By accurately completing Form 1120S, providing shareholders with Schedule K-1, and fulfilling any other necessary tax obligations, you can avoid penalties and ensure your business operates smoothly.

In the next chapter, we will explore effective tax strategies for S-Corps, allowing you to maximize deductions and minimize tax liabilities, further enhancing your business's financial health.

Chapter 10: Tax Strategies for S-Corps

Effectively managing your tax obligations is crucial for the success of your LLC S-Corp.

This chapter delves into strategic approaches to minimize self-employment taxes, maximize deductions, and avoid common tax pitfalls.

By understanding these strategies, you can enhance your business's financial health and keep more of your hard-earned money.

Minimizing Self-Employment Tax

Understanding Self-Employment Tax

Self-employment tax is a combination of Social Security and Medicare taxes that self-employed individuals must pay on their earnings.

For S-Corp shareholders who actively work in the business, it's essential to navigate self-employment tax carefully.

How to Minimize It

One of the primary benefits of an S-Corp is the potential to minimize self-employment tax liability. Here's how:

Reasonable Salary vs. Distributions: As an S-Corp owner, you must pay yourself a reasonable salary for the work you perform.

However, any additional profits can be distributed as dividends to shareholders. These dividends are not subject to self-employment tax.

Therefore, by balancing your salary and distributions, you can minimize the amount subject to self-employment tax while still complying with IRS regulations.

Set a Reasonable Salary: The IRS requires that S-Corp owners take a reasonable salary, which is based on what similar businesses pay for similar services.

This means you should research industry standards to determine what a fair salary would be for your role.

Setting a salary too low can raise red flags with the IRS, while a salary that is too high can lead to unnecessary tax payments.

Maximizing Deductions

The Importance of Deductions

Deductions lower your taxable income, ultimately reducing the amount of tax you owe. S-Corps enjoy various deductible business expenses, which can significantly impact your overall tax liability.

Common Deductions for S-Corps

Here are some key deductions to consider:

Business Expenses: Any ordinary and necessary expenses directly related to the operation of your business are deductible. This includes costs such as office supplies, equipment, and business travel.

Employee Salaries and Benefits: Salaries paid to employees, including yourself as the owner, are deductible expenses.

Additionally, contributions to retirement plans and employee benefits like health insurance premiums can also be deducted.

Home Office Deduction: If you operate your business from home, you may be eligible for a home office deduction.

This deduction allows you to write off a portion of your home expenses, such as rent, mortgage interest, utilities, and repairs, based on the space used for business purposes.

Depreciation: If your S-Corp purchases significant assets like equipment or vehicles, you can deduct the depreciation over time.

This allows you to spread the cost of these assets over their useful lives, lowering your taxable income each year.

Record Keeping

To maximize deductions, maintain meticulous records of all business expenses. This includes receipts, invoices, and documentation that supports your deductions, as the IRS may request proof during an audit.

Avoiding Common Tax Pitfalls

Understanding Tax Pitfalls

Being aware of potential tax pitfalls can save you from costly mistakes and unnecessary penalties. Here are some common issues S-Corp owners encounter:

Failing to Pay a Reasonable Salary: As mentioned earlier, not paying yourself a reasonable salary can trigger IRS scrutiny. Ensure that your salary reflects the industry standards for your role to avoid penalties.

Mixing Personal and Business Expenses: It's essential to keep personal and business finances separate.

Mixing expenses can lead to complications during tax filing and may raise red flags with the IRS.

Open a separate bank account for your business and use it exclusively for business-related transactions.

Neglecting to File Required Forms: Missing deadlines or failing to file required tax forms, such as Form 1120S or Schedule K-1, can result in penalties and interest.

Create a calendar with due dates and set reminders to ensure timely filing.

Ignoring State and Local Taxes: Don't overlook state and local tax obligations. Some states may impose additional taxes on S-Corps, so ensure you're aware of your state's specific requirements and deadlines.

Conclusion

Implementing effective tax strategies is vital for the financial success of your LLC S-Corp.

By minimizing self-employment taxes, maximizing deductions, and avoiding common pitfalls, you can improve your bottom line and ensure compliance with tax regulations.

In the next chapter, we will explore the specific tax filing requirements for S-Corps, including the necessary forms and deadlines, to help you stay organized and compliant with your tax obligations.

Part 4: Compliance and Maintenance

Chapter 11: Maintaining S-Corp Status

Maintaining your S-Corp status is crucial for enjoying the tax benefits and protections it offers.

This chapter outlines the key steps you must take to keep your S-Corp in good standing, including annual reporting requirements, compliance with tax laws, and best practices for record-keeping.

Annual Reporting Requirements

Understanding Annual Reports

Most states require S-Corps to file an annual report to maintain good standing. This report typically includes basic information about the business, such as its address, registered agent, and management structure.

What You Need to Do

Check State Requirements: The requirements for annual reports vary by state. Some states require detailed information about your business activities, while others may have simpler forms.

Make sure to check your state's specific requirements to ensure compliance.

Filing Deadlines: Be aware of the filing deadlines for your annual report. Missing the deadline may result in penalties, late fees, or even the loss of your S-Corp status.

Set reminders on your calendar to keep track of these important dates.

Fees: There is usually a fee associated with filing your annual report. Ensure you budget for this expense and pay it on time to avoid any complications.

Compliance with Tax Laws

Staying Compliant

To maintain your S-Corp status, you must comply with federal, state, and local tax laws. This involves not only filing the required forms but also adhering to tax regulations throughout the year.

Key Compliance Tasks

Filing Form 1120S: As an S-Corp, you are required to file Form 1120S annually. This form reports the income, deductions, gains, and losses of your corporation.

Ensure that you file this form by the due date, which is typically March 15 for most businesses.

Providing Schedule K-1: Along with Form 1120S, you must issue Schedule K-1 to each shareholder.

This form outlines each shareholder's share of the corporation's income, deductions, and credits. It's essential to provide accurate information, as shareholders will use this to report their income on their personal tax returns.

Understanding Employment Tax Obligations: If your S-Corp has employees, you must comply with federal and state employment tax laws.

This includes withholding income taxes, Social Security, and Medicare taxes from employees' paychecks, as well as paying the employer's portion of these taxes.

Record-Keeping Best Practices

Importance of Good Record-Keeping

Proper record-keeping is vital for maintaining your S-Corp status and ensuring compliance with tax laws. It also helps you manage your business effectively and prepare for potential audits.

Best Practices for Record-Keeping

Maintain Separate Accounts: Keep your business and personal finances separate by using a dedicated business bank account. This simplifies tracking income and expenses and helps avoid issues with the IRS.

Organize Financial Records: Set up a system for organizing financial documents, such as receipts, invoices, and bank statements.

Use accounting software or spreadsheets to track your income and expenses systematically.

Document Important Decisions: Keep written records of important business decisions, such as changes in ownership, updates to your operating agreement, and significant financial transactions.

This documentation provides clarity and can be helpful if questions arise in the future.

Store Records Safely: Store your records in a secure location, whether physical or digital. Consider backing up important documents in the cloud to protect them from loss due to fire, theft, or other unforeseen circumstances.

Conclusion

Maintaining S-Corp status requires diligence in fulfilling annual reporting requirements, ensuring compliance with tax laws, and implementing effective record-keeping practices.

By staying organized and proactive, you can protect your business and continue to enjoy the benefits that come with being an S-Corp.

In the next chapter, we will explore how to handle changes in ownership and management within your S-Corp, including the necessary steps for adding or removing owners and amending the operating agreement.

Chapter 12: Handling Changes in Ownership and Management

Change is a natural part of any business, and handling changes in ownership and management within your S-Corp is essential for maintaining stability and compliance.

This chapter discusses the steps involved in adding or removing owners, changing the management structure, and amending the operating agreement.

Adding or Removing Owners

Understanding Ownership Changes

Ownership changes can occur for various reasons, such as bringing in new partners for capital, expertise, or a shift in business strategy.

It's crucial to handle these changes carefully to maintain compliance with both legal and tax obligations.

Steps for Adding Owners

Review Eligibility: Ensure that the new owner meets the eligibility requirements for S-Corp status.

The IRS has specific restrictions on who can be a shareholder, including limits on the number of shareholders and who can own shares.

Determine Share Allocation: Decide how many shares the new owner will receive and at what value.

This may involve adjusting the ownership percentages of existing owners, so communicate transparently about the changes.

Update the Operating Agreement: After the new owner is added, update your operating agreement to reflect the change in ownership structure.

This document should outline the roles and responsibilities of the new owner and any changes to decision-making processes.

Steps for Removing Owners

Evaluate the Reasons: Understand why the owner is being removed—whether due to personal reasons, performance issues, or strategic shifts. This evaluation can guide the process and ensure it's handled professionally.

Consult the Operating Agreement: Refer to your operating agreement for specific procedures regarding the removal of an owner. This may include buyout provisions or notice requirements.

Finalize the Buyout: If applicable, negotiate a buyout agreement with the departing owner. This should outline the compensation they will receive for their shares and the timeline for the transaction.

Changing Management Structure

When to Change Management

Changes in management structure may be necessary for a variety of reasons, such as business growth, shifts in strategic direction, or the need for new skills and expertise.

Steps to Change Management

Assess Current Management Needs: Evaluate whether the current management team aligns with your business goals. Consider whether new roles or responsibilities need to be created.

Communicate with Stakeholders: Inform all stakeholders—owners, employees, and potentially clients—about changes in management. Transparency fosters trust and helps ensure a smooth transition.

Update Management Roles: Clearly define the new roles and responsibilities of each manager. This clarity helps prevent confusion and ensures everyone understands their contributions to the business.

Document Changes: Keep written records of any changes to the management structure. This documentation can be helpful for future reference and may be necessary for compliance purposes.

Amending the Operating Agreement

Importance of the Operating Agreement

Your operating agreement is a foundational document that outlines the rules and procedures for your S-Corp, including ownership, management, and operational guidelines.

Amending this agreement when changes occur is essential for maintaining legal compliance.

Steps to Amend the Operating Agreement

Draft the Amendment: Create a formal amendment that specifies what changes are being made, such as adding or removing owners and updating management responsibilities.

Obtain Consensus: Depending on your operating agreement, you may need approval from a majority or all of the owners to make amendments. Discuss the changes openly to gain consensus and address any concerns.

Sign and Date the Amendment: Once agreed upon, ensure that all relevant parties sign and date the amendment. This creates a legal record of the changes made to the operating agreement.

Distribute Updated Copies: Share the amended operating agreement with all owners and managers.

Keeping everyone informed helps ensure that everyone is on the same page regarding the rules and procedures.

Conclusion

Handling changes in ownership and management requires careful planning and clear communication.

By following the appropriate steps to add or remove owners, adjust the management structure, and amend the operating agreement, you can ensure that your S-Corp remains compliant and continues to operate smoothly.

In the next chapter, we will explore the process of dissolving an LLC S-Corp, including the reasons for dissolution and the necessary steps to take.

Chapter 13: Dissolving an LLC S-Corp

Dissolving an LLC S-Corp is a significant decision that requires careful consideration and adherence to specific legal and financial procedures.

Whether the dissolution is due to business closure, mergers, or other reasons, understanding the reasons for dissolution, the step-by-step process, and post-dissolution obligations is crucial to ensure everything is handled correctly.

Reasons for Dissolution

There are many reasons why an LLC S-Corp might be dissolved, and it's important to evaluate the situation carefully to ensure that dissolution is the right course of action.

Common Reasons for Dissolution

Voluntary Closure: The owners or shareholders may decide to close the business due to retirement, a shift in priorities, or financial underperformance. In such cases, it's a proactive decision made by the owners.

Merger or Acquisition: When a business is acquired by another entity or merges with another company, the original LLC S-Corp may need to be dissolved as part of the restructuring process.

Bankruptcy or Insolvency: Financial hardship may lead a business to file for bankruptcy, making dissolution a necessary outcome if the company is unable to recover.

Disagreements Among Owners: Sometimes, irreconcilable differences between owners may result in the decision to dissolve the business.

Legal or Compliance Issues: Failing to comply with state or federal regulations or incurring legal liabilities might force the business to dissolve.

Step-by-Step Dissolution Process

Once the decision to dissolve an LLC S-Corp has been made, there is a formal process that must be followed to properly wind down the business.

Skipping steps or failing to follow legal procedures can result in complications or ongoing liabilities.

Step-by-Step Dissolution Process

Vote for Dissolution: Owners or shareholders must vote to dissolve the LLC S-Corp, typically following the rules outlined in the operating agreement.

The agreement may require a majority vote or unanimous consent.

File Articles of Dissolution: After the decision to dissolve has been made, you'll need to file articles of dissolution with the state where your LLC S-Corp was formed.

This officially notifies the state that the business is closing.

Notify Creditors: You must inform all creditors of your intent to dissolve the LLC S-Corp. This gives them an opportunity to file any claims or request payments for outstanding debts.

Settle Debts and Obligations: Pay off any remaining business debts or liabilities. This may involve liquidating assets to cover outstanding obligations.

Distribute Remaining Assets: After debts are settled, distribute any remaining assets to the owners or shareholders according to the terms of the operating agreement.

Cancel Business Licenses and Permits: Ensure that any business licenses, permits, or registrations (such as your EIN) are canceled with the appropriate authorities.

Final Tax Filings: File your final federal and state tax returns. You may need to file a final Form 1120S (for S-Corp taxes) and close any accounts related to sales tax, payroll tax, and other tax obligations.

Close Business Bank Accounts: Once all financial obligations have been met and assets distributed, close the business's bank accounts and any lines of credit associated with the LLC S-Corp.

Post-Dissolution Obligations

Even after the LLC S-Corp is dissolved, there are a few remaining obligations to take care of to ensure that the dissolution is complete and that there are no lingering liabilities.

Post-Dissolution Responsibilities

Maintain Records: Even after dissolution, it's important to keep business records, including tax filings, financial statements, and dissolution documents, for several years (usually at least 3 to 7 years).

This can help resolve any legal, tax, or financial questions that arise later.

Follow Up with Creditors and Tax Authorities: After settling debts and filing taxes, continue to monitor for any notices or follow-up actions required from creditors or tax authorities.

Sometimes, a creditor may file a claim after the business has been dissolved, and it's important to address such claims promptly.

Personal Tax Liabilities: Depending on how assets were distributed, owners may face personal tax obligations from the dissolution of the LLC S-Corp.

It's important to consult with a tax professional to understand any personal tax consequences.

Conclusion

Dissolving an LLC S-Corp involves multiple steps, from voting on the decision to closing business accounts and fulfilling tax obligations.

By following the correct dissolution process and managing post-dissolution responsibilities, owners can ensure that the business is wound down smoothly without leaving any loose ends.

In the next chapter, we will dive into managing the finances and cash flow of an S-Corp to ensure continued business success.

Part 5: Day-to-Day Operations

Chapter 14: Managing Finances and Cash Flow

Managing the finances and cash flow of your LLC S-Corp is critical to its long-term success.

Whether you're just starting out or have been in business for years, understanding how to budget, forecast, manage accounts receivable and payable, and maintain healthy cash flow will help you stay in control of your business's financial health.

In this chapter, we'll explore practical steps and strategies to keep your LLC S-Corp financially stable and prepared for future growth.

Budgeting and Forecasting

Budgeting and forecasting are essential tools for planning and ensuring that your business stays on track financially.

A budget is a plan for how your business will spend and save money, while forecasting involves predicting future revenue and expenses based on current trends.

Creating a Budget

Start with Revenue Projections: Estimate how much income your business is likely to generate over a specific period (monthly, quarterly, or annually).

Consider past sales data, market trends, and any new contracts or clients you expect to acquire.

Identify Fixed and Variable Expenses: Fixed expenses, such as rent, salaries, and insurance, stay the same each month, while variable expenses (such as utilities, supplies, or travel) may fluctuate.

Plan for Unexpected Costs: Set aside a portion of your budget for unexpected expenses. This is your financial safety net in case of emergencies or sudden changes in the market.

Forecasting Future Performance

Use Historical Data: Look at past financial statements to identify trends in revenue and expenses. This will help you create realistic forecasts for future growth or challenges.

Adjust for Seasonality: Some businesses have seasonal peaks and dips. Account for these fluctuations when forecasting so that you can prepare for slower periods.

Budgeting and forecasting provide a financial roadmap for your business. They help you allocate resources effectively and make informed decisions about growth, investments, and other important areas.

Managing Accounts Receivable and Payable

Efficiently managing accounts receivable (AR) and accounts payable (AP) is essential for maintaining steady cash flow.

These two areas represent the money that your business earns and the money it owes.

Managing Accounts Receivable (AR)

Set Clear Payment Terms: Establish standard payment terms (e.g., Net 30 or Net 60) and communicate them clearly to your clients. This sets expectations for when payments are due.

Follow Up on Invoices: Regularly review unpaid invoices and follow up with clients who are late in making payments. Offering discounts for early payments or charging late fees can encourage timely payments.

Offer Multiple Payment Methods: Providing clients with different ways to pay (credit cards, bank transfers, etc.) can make it easier for them to pay on time.

Managing Accounts Payable (AP)

Track Due Dates: Make sure you know when your bills and expenses are due. Missing payments can hurt your business's credit score and relationships with suppliers.

Negotiate with Vendors: Try to negotiate favorable terms with vendors, such as extended payment deadlines or discounts for early payments.

Automate Payments: Automating recurring payments can help ensure that bills are paid on time, reducing the risk of late fees or penalties.

Effectively managing AR and AP helps you avoid cash flow problems and keeps your business running smoothly by ensuring that money is coming in when it's needed and going out in an organized manner.

Cash Flow Management Strategies

Cash flow is the lifeblood of your business. Even profitable companies can fail if they don't have enough cash on hand to pay bills and meet day-to-day financial obligations.

To maintain positive cash flow, it's important to implement smart management strategies.

Strategies for Improving Cash Flow

Monitor Cash Flow Regularly: Keep a close eye on your cash flow by reviewing your financial statements regularly. This helps you spot any potential problems before they escalate.

Maintain a Cash Reserve: Having a cash reserve (savings) is crucial for covering expenses during slow periods. Aim to have enough cash on hand to cover at least three to six months of operating expenses.

Speed Up Invoicing: Don't delay sending out invoices. The sooner you invoice clients, the sooner you can collect payment. Automating invoicing systems can also help streamline the process.

Control Spending: Carefully track and control your business expenses. Avoid unnecessary spending, and look for areas where you can cut costs without sacrificing quality.

Use a Line of Credit: Having access to a line of credit can provide your business with extra cash when needed. This can be especially helpful during short-term cash crunches.

Maintaining a steady cash flow requires ongoing attention and proactive management. By implementing smart strategies and regularly monitoring your finances, you can ensure that your business remains financially healthy and prepared for future opportunities or challenges.

Conclusion

Managing finances and cash flow is a cornerstone of running a successful LLC S-Corp.

Through careful budgeting, forecasting, and managing your accounts receivable and payable, you can ensure financial stability and be prepared for both opportunities and challenges.

Implementing effective cash flow strategies will help keep your business running smoothly, no matter what the future holds.

In the next chapter, we'll explore how to effectively hire and manage employees to support your business's day-to-day operations.

Chapter 15: Hiring and Managing Employees

Employees are the backbone of any business, and the success of your LLC S-Corp depends greatly on finding the right people and managing them effectively.

Whether you're hiring your first employee or expanding your team, recruitment, employee benefits, compensation, and managing the separation process are key to creating a positive and productive work environment.

In this chapter, we'll walk through how to recruit top talent, structure employee benefits and compensation packages, and handle employee termination with professionalism and care.

Recruitment and Hiring

Hiring the right employees is essential for the growth of your business. Effective recruitment involves attracting, selecting, and onboarding candidates who have the right skills and fit well within your company culture.

Steps for Effective Recruitment

Define the Role: Before you start recruiting, clearly define the responsibilities, qualifications, and expectations for the role. A well-crafted job description helps attract the right candidates.

Advertise the Position: Use a mix of online job boards, social media, and professional networks to promote the job opening. You can also leverage referrals from current employees or industry contacts.

Screen Candidates: Review resumes and cover letters to shortlist candidates who meet the qualifications. Conduct phone or video interviews as an initial screening step.

Interviewing: When interviewing candidates, ask open-ended questions to gauge their experience, problem-solving abilities, and cultural fit. Use a mix of behavioral and technical questions to assess their competency.

Reference Checks: After narrowing down your choices, conduct reference checks to verify the candidate's work history, skills, and professionalism.

Onboarding: Once you've hired the candidate, provide a structured onboarding process to help them acclimate to the company. Introduce them to the team, explain company policies, and provide any necessary training.

A well-organized recruitment process ensures that you bring on employees who will contribute positively to your business and align with your company's long-term goals.

Employee Benefits and Compensation

Offering competitive employee benefits and fair compensation is essential for attracting and retaining top talent.

Compensation goes beyond salary—benefits can include health insurance, retirement plans, paid time off, and more.

Structuring Compensation

Determine Salaries: Set competitive salary ranges based on industry standards, location, and the role's responsibilities. Regularly review and adjust salaries to remain competitive in the job market.

Performance-Based Pay: Consider offering performance-based incentives such as bonuses or commissions to motivate employees and reward exceptional work.

Employee Benefits

Health Insurance: Providing health benefits is a major incentive for employees. You can offer various plans, such as medical, dental, and vision coverage.

Retirement Plans: Offering a retirement plan like a 401(k) with employer matching can help employees save for the future and increase loyalty to your company.

Paid Time Off (PTO): Give employees paid leave for vacation, personal days, and sick time. Flexible PTO policies are attractive to potential hires.

Other Perks: Consider offering additional benefits like wellness programs, gym memberships, or remote work options. These perks can enhance job satisfaction and improve employee retention.

Balancing competitive salaries and thoughtful benefits shows your employees that you value their contributions and well-being. It also reduces turnover and helps maintain a motivated workforce.

Termination and Separation

Employee termination, whether voluntary or involuntary, can be a sensitive issue.

Handling separations with professionalism and compassion is crucial to maintaining a positive reputation for your business and ensuring that legal obligations are met.

Termination and Separation Process

Voluntary Termination: When an employee resigns, ask for a formal resignation letter and conduct an exit interview to gather feedback on their experience with the company.

This can provide valuable insights for improving workplace culture.

Involuntary Termination: If you need to terminate an employee due to performance issues or misconduct, follow a fair and documented process.

Ensure the employee has been given clear feedback, warnings, and an opportunity to improve before termination. This protects your business from potential legal issues.

Severance and Final Pay: Depending on the circumstances of the termination, you may offer a severance package, especially for long-term employees.

Also, ensure that the employee receives their final paycheck, including any accrued vacation days, as required by law.

Handle with Dignity: Always terminate employees with respect and professionalism. Provide them with information about benefits continuation (such as COBRA for health insurance), and assist with transitioning out of the company, if possible.

Managing employee separations respectfully helps protect your business from legal challenges and preserves your professional reputation.

It also allows the remaining team members to continue their work without disruption.

Conclusion

Hiring, managing, and even parting ways with employees are fundamental aspects of running an LLC S-Corp.

Building a strong recruitment process ensures that you bring in the right people, while offering competitive compensation and benefits keeps your team engaged and loyal.

Finally, handling employee terminations with care and professionalism is critical for maintaining your company's integrity.

In the next chapter, we'll dive into how to maintain proper business records and stay compliant with regulatory requirements, ensuring that your LLC S-Corp operates smoothly and legally.

Chapter 16: Maintaining Business Records and Compliance

Running an LLC S-Corp requires diligent record-keeping and strict adherence to various regulatory requirements.

Keeping accurate records helps you track your company's financial health, prepare for tax season, and ensure compliance with state and federal regulations.

This chapter will walk you through essential record-keeping requirements, document retention policies, and tips for staying compliant with relevant laws.

Record-Keeping Requirements

Proper record-keeping is critical for any business, especially an LLC S-Corp.

Your business records provide a clear picture of financial transactions, business activities, and legal obligations.

Organized records are necessary not only for internal management but also for tax filings, audits, and legal compliance.

Key Records to Maintain

Financial Records: This includes income statements, balance sheets, profit and loss statements, and general ledgers.

These documents are essential for tracking income and expenses, which are required for tax reporting.

Tax Records: Keep copies of all tax returns and supporting documents, such as receipts, invoices, payroll records, and sales tax filings.

Operating Agreement and Formation Documents: Retain a copy of your LLC's Articles of Organization, Operating Agreement, and any amendments. These documents outline how your business is structured and governed.

Meeting Minutes: If your LLC S-Corp holds formal meetings (e.g., board or shareholder meetings), record the minutes of these meetings.

These serve as legal proof of business decisions and actions taken by management or ownership.

Contracts and Agreements: Keep records of all contracts, leases, employment agreements, and other legal documents related to your business.

Permits and Licenses: Maintain current copies of all business licenses and permits required by your industry or location.

Keeping these records organized and accessible ensures that you have all necessary documentation on hand for tax filing, audits, or any legal challenges that may arise.

Document Retention Policies

Not all records need to be kept forever, but certain documents must be retained for specific periods to comply with legal requirements.

Having a document retention policy ensures that you manage your records efficiently while staying compliant with laws.

General Retention Guidelines

Tax Records: Retain federal and state tax returns, along with all supporting documents, for at least seven years. This includes receipts, payroll records, and any correspondence with tax authorities.

Financial Records: Keep financial statements, bank statements, and accounting records for at least seven years.

Employment Records: Maintain personnel records, including employment contracts, benefits information, and payroll records, for at least four to seven years after an employee's termination.

Corporate Documents: Formation documents, meeting minutes, and major contracts should be kept indefinitely, as they establish your business's structure and legal agreements.

Legal Documents: Any contracts, agreements, or legal documents related to business operations should be kept for at least the duration of the contract and a few years after it expires or is terminated.

By following a clear document retention policy, you ensure that you're prepared for any audits, disputes, or legal challenges.

It also helps you avoid keeping unnecessary records, saving storage space and reducing clutter.

Compliance with Regulatory Requirements

Compliance refers to adhering to all applicable laws, rules, and regulations governing your business.

LLC S-Corps must comply with both federal and state regulations, including annual filings, tax obligations, and record-keeping laws.

Common Compliance Requirements

Annual Reports: Many states require LLCs and S-Corps to file annual reports or statements that update the state on the business's key information, such as ownership and address.

These reports are typically due on the anniversary of the company's formation or at the end of the fiscal year.

Taxes: In addition to filing your federal and state income tax returns, LLC S-Corps must comply with payroll tax laws, sales tax regulations, and any other applicable taxes.

Make sure to stay on top of tax deadlines to avoid penalties.

Employment Laws: If your business has employees, ensure that you comply with employment laws, including wage and hour regulations, worker's compensation, and workplace safety laws.

Permits and Licenses: Stay up to date with renewing any necessary permits or licenses. Failing to do so could result in fines or the inability to legally operate your business.

S-Corp Election: To maintain S-Corp status, you must ensure you continue to meet the IRS's eligibility requirements, including restrictions on ownership and the type of shareholders.

Regularly review your business's compliance status to ensure that you are meeting all legal obligations. Staying compliant will help protect your business from fines, penalties, or even dissolution.

Conclusion

Maintaining proper business records and ensuring compliance are critical to the long-term success and stability of your LLC S-Corp.

Accurate and organized records not only help you manage your business more effectively, but they are also essential for staying compliant with tax laws and regulatory requirements.

By implementing a strong record-keeping system and following a clear document retention policy, you can keep your business on track and avoid potential legal issues.

Part 6: Advanced Topics and Best Practices

Chapter 17: Advanced Tax Strategies

As your LLC S-Corp grows, you may find that basic tax strategies are no longer enough to maximize your tax savings.

Advanced tax strategies can help you minimize your tax burden, increase deductions, and strategically reinvest in your business.

In this chapter, we will explore key advanced tax strategies, including Section 179 deductions, bonus depreciation, and other methods for reducing taxable income.

Section 179 Deductions

What is Section 179? Section 179 of the IRS tax code allows businesses to deduct the full purchase price of qualifying equipment or software in the year it was purchased, rather than depreciating it over several years.

This is especially beneficial for small businesses that need to invest in assets like machinery, office furniture, or business vehicles.

The goal of Section 179 is to encourage businesses to invest in themselves by allowing immediate tax relief.

How Does It Work? Under Section 179, your LLC S-Corp can deduct up to a certain limit (set annually by the IRS) of qualifying equipment costs in the year you place the equipment into service.

For example, if your business purchases $50,000 worth of office equipment, you can deduct the full amount from your taxable income in that tax year, reducing your overall tax liability.

Key Considerations

Qualifying Property: Not all purchases qualify for Section 179. Common eligible items include office furniture, business vehicles, machinery, computers, and software used for business operations.

Annual Limits: The IRS sets annual limits for Section 179 deductions. For example, in 2024, the limit was $1,160,000, but this amount may vary yearly based on inflation adjustments.

Income Limitation: You cannot use Section 179 deductions to create a loss. The deduction is limited to the total taxable income your business earns in the year, so it's best used in profitable years.

Section 179 deductions allow you to deduct large expenses immediately, making it a powerful tool for businesses that need to invest in equipment to grow.

Bonus Depreciation

What is Bonus Depreciation? Bonus depreciation is another way to deduct the cost of business assets, but it operates differently from Section 179.

While Section 179 allows for immediate deductions up to a specific limit, bonus depreciation allows businesses to deduct a percentage of the cost of qualifying assets immediately, with no cap on the amount that can be claimed.

This makes it particularly useful for larger businesses or those with significant capital expenditures.

How Does It Work? For assets purchased and placed in service, the IRS allows a specific percentage of the purchase cost to be deducted upfront.

Currently, businesses can deduct 80% of the cost of qualifying assets in the first year, with the remaining amount depreciated over time. This percentage was previously set at 100% but is gradually being phased down (from 2023 onward).

Key Considerations

Qualifying Assets: Like Section 179, bonus depreciation applies to tangible business property, such as machinery, equipment, and some software.

However, it also applies to improvements made to existing property, such as roofing or security systems.

No Income Limitations: Unlike Section 179, bonus depreciation can be used even if it creates a loss. This makes it particularly attractive for businesses that are investing heavily in growth or expansion.

Combining with Section 179: Businesses can combine Section 179 and bonus depreciation.

First, they use Section 179 to deduct the maximum allowed and then apply bonus depreciation to the remaining amount.

Bonus depreciation is a flexible tax-saving tool, especially valuable for companies with significant capital investments that exceed Section 179 limits.

Other Advanced Tax Strategies

Beyond Section 179 and bonus depreciation, there are other advanced tax strategies that can help your LLC S-Corp reduce its tax liability:

Retirement Plan Contributions: One way to reduce taxable income while benefiting yourself and your employees is by contributing to retirement plans.

As a business owner, you can establish a retirement plan for your employees (e.g., a 401(k) or SEP IRA) and deduct the contributions your business makes to these plans.

This provides a tax benefit while also improving employee retention and morale.

Health Insurance Deductions: If your LLC S-Corp provides health insurance for its employees, you may be eligible for a small business health care tax credit.

Additionally, if you're an owner-employee and your S-Corp pays for your health insurance, those premiums are deductible on the business's tax return, reducing overall taxable income.

Hiring Incentives and Credits: The IRS offers various tax credits for hiring employees from certain groups, such as veterans, long-term unemployed individuals, or people with disabilities.

The Work Opportunity Tax Credit (WOTC): This credit can provide significant savings while allowing your business to give back to the community by hiring individuals from underrepresented groups.

Research and Development (R&D) Tax Credits: If your LLC S-Corp is involved in developing new products, processes, or services, you may qualify for the R&D tax credit.

This credit is designed to encourage innovation and can significantly reduce your tax liability if you're investing in research and development activities.

Conclusion

Advanced tax strategies like Section 179 deductions, bonus depreciation, and other techniques can significantly reduce your LLC S-Corp taxable income and provide valuable financial relief.

By taking advantage of these strategies, you can reinvest savings back into your business and fuel future growth.

As your LLC S-Corp continues to expand, it's essential to stay informed about changing tax laws and work with a tax professional to ensure you're making the most of these opportunities.

The next chapter will focus on strategies for business growth and expansion, helping you take your company to the next level.

Chapter 18: Business Growth and Expansion

Growth is a natural and exciting phase for any successful LLC S-Corp.

Whether you're looking to increase revenue, expand into new markets, or grow your team, business expansion presents opportunities as well as challenges.

In this chapter, we'll explore strategies for achieving sustainable growth, managing the complexities of expansion, and avoiding common pitfalls that could derail your progress.

Strategies for Growth

Expanding Product or Service Offerings: One of the most effective ways to grow your business is by expanding your product or service offerings.

Look for gaps in the market or areas where your business could provide additional value to customers.

This might involve introducing new products that complement your current offerings or expanding into related services.

Before introducing new products, conduct thorough market research to ensure there is demand and to understand how to position them effectively.

Entering New Markets: If your business has found success in one market, consider expanding into new geographic areas or demographics.

This could mean opening new locations, launching your online presence internationally, or targeting different customer segments.

Expanding into new markets can diversify your revenue streams and reduce dependency on one location or demographic.

However, it requires careful planning, market analysis, and often additional resources.

Investing in Marketing and Branding Growth: This involves building a strong brand and expanding your customer base through targeted marketing efforts.

Investing in digital marketing strategies, such as social media advertising, search engine optimization (SEO), and email marketing campaigns, can help you reach new customers and retain existing ones.

Building brand recognition and customer loyalty through consistent messaging and excellent customer service will further fuel growth.

Mergers and Acquisitions: Another option for growth is acquiring other businesses or merging with a company that complements yours.

This strategy can provide immediate access to new customers, markets, and resources. Mergers and acquisitions can be complex, so ensure you perform thorough due diligence and consult with legal and financial experts before making any decisions.

Managing Expansion

Scaling Your Operations: As your business grows, scaling your operations is crucial to ensuring that you can meet increased demand without sacrificing quality or efficiency.

This might involve automating certain processes, hiring additional staff, or upgrading your technology systems. Creating scalable systems early on will help your business handle growth smoothly.

Building a Strong Leadership Team: As your business expands, leadership becomes increasingly important.

You may not be able to oversee every aspect of the business as you once did, so it's essential to build a leadership team you can trust.

Delegate responsibilities to capable managers and make sure you have the right team in place to lead different departments, from operations and finance to sales and marketing.

Strong leadership is key to ensuring your business continues to run smoothly during periods of growth.

Maintaining Cash Flow Growth: This often requires significant upfront investments, whether it's in inventory, equipment, marketing, or hiring.

Managing your cash flow becomes critical during expansion. Make sure you have enough working capital to support your growth plans without overextending yourself financially.

You may need to explore financing options, such as business loans or lines of credit, to ensure you have the cash flow needed for expansion.

Avoiding Common Pitfalls

Overexpansion: One of the most common mistakes businesses make during periods of growth is expanding too quickly.

While growth is exciting, moving too fast can lead to overextension, both financially and operationally. Ensure that each phase of your expansion is backed by thorough market research, financial projections, and a clear plan for execution.

Expanding too quickly without the necessary infrastructure can lead to issues like cash flow shortages, supply chain problems, or a decline in customer service quality.

Losing Focus on Core Business: As you grow, it can be tempting to branch out into too many areas.

While diversification is important, it's essential not to lose sight of your core business. Stay focused on what made your business successful in the first place, and ensure that your new ventures complement your existing offerings rather than distracting from them.

Keep refining and improving your core products or services even as you expand.

Neglecting Company Culture: Rapid growth can strain your company culture. As you hire more employees and open new locations, maintaining the same level of communication, teamwork, and shared values can become challenging.

It's important to nurture your company culture during expansion to ensure that new hires align with your values and that your current employees remain engaged and motivated.

Regularly communicate with your team, provide opportunities for professional development, and foster a positive work environment.

Conclusion

Expanding your LLC S-Corp is an exciting step that can lead to increased revenue, market share, and long-term success.

However, growth must be managed carefully to avoid pitfalls like overexpansion or losing focus on your core business.

By developing clear strategies for growth, building a strong leadership team, and maintaining financial discipline, you can successfully navigate the challenges of business expansion.

Chapter 19: Best Practices for LLC S-Corps

Running an LLC S-Corp efficiently involves more than just maintaining compliance and keeping the books balanced.

To ensure long-term success, it's essential to implement best practices that guide governance, manage risks, and prepare for the future.

In this chapter, we will cover the key areas of governance, risk management, and succession planning, and how applying best practices in these areas will help your LLC S-Corp thrive.

Governance and Decision-Making

Establishing a Governance Structure In an LLC S-Corp, effective governance begins with having a clear structure for decision-making and management.

This often includes defining the roles of owners, managers, and any board of directors.

A well-structured governance system ensures that all business decisions are made with transparency and accountability, reducing the risk of miscommunication or conflicts between stakeholders.

Operating Agreement as a Governance Tool: Your LLC's operating agreement plays a crucial role in governance.

This legal document outlines how decisions are made, who has the authority to make them, and how profits and losses are distributed.

For example, the agreement may state whether decisions are made by majority vote or unanimous consent, and how day-to-day management responsibilities are assigned.

It's important to regularly review and update your operating agreement to reflect the current structure and needs of your business.

Facilitating Effective Communication: Open and clear communication between members, managers, and employees is essential for good governance.

Regular meetings, whether formal or informal, help ensure that everyone is on the same page and aware of the company's goals and any challenges.

For larger LLC S-Corps, having an advisory board can provide additional oversight and guidance on major decisions.

Risk Management

Identifying Business Risks Every business faces risks, and managing these risks effectively is key to long-term success.

Common risks for LLC S-Corps include financial risks, such as cash flow shortages or unexpected expenses, as well as operational risks, like supply chain disruptions or employee turnover.

Additionally, legal and regulatory risks, such as lawsuits or compliance failures, can threaten your business.

Insurance and Liability Protection: One of the primary reasons for forming an LLC is to protect personal assets from business liabilities. However, it's important to back up this legal protection with adequate insurance coverage.

Consider liability insurance, property insurance, and workers' compensation to protect your LLC S-Corp from financial loss in the event of an accident, lawsuit, or other unforeseen events.

Regularly review your insurance policies to ensure they cover your business's evolving needs.

Risk Mitigation Strategies: In addition to insurance, there are several risk mitigation strategies you can implement.

These include diversifying your revenue streams, maintaining emergency cash reserves, and creating contingency plans for various potential disruptions.

For example, if a key supplier fails, having alternative suppliers lined up can prevent delays in production. If a key employee leaves, having a succession plan in place ensures that the business continues to operate smoothly.

Compliance as a Risk Management Tool: Ensuring that your LLC S-Corp remains compliant with state and federal laws is another essential aspect of risk management.

This includes staying up-to-date on tax laws, filing necessary paperwork on time, and adhering to employment regulations.

Failing to maintain compliance can result in fines, penalties, or even the loss of your S-Corp status, so it's important to prioritize this aspect of risk management.

Succession Planning

Why Succession Planning Matters At some point, every business owner must plan for the future, whether that means retiring, selling the business, or stepping aside for new leadership.

Succession planning ensures a smooth transition when the time comes. Without a clear plan, your LLC S-Corp may face disruption, confusion, or even closure if key leadership roles are left vacant or passed on without proper preparation.

Choosing Successors: One of the most important parts of succession planning is identifying and grooming successors.

This may be a family member, a trusted employee, or an outside buyer. If you plan to keep the business within the family, start discussing your plans with potential heirs early to ensure they are prepared and willing to take on the responsibility.

If succession involves selling the business, begin evaluating potential buyers and considering the terms of the sale well in advance.

Preparing for Leadership Transition: Once successors are identified, they should be given opportunities to gain experience and understand the inner workings of the business.

This might include mentoring, leadership training, or gradually increasing their responsibilities within the LLC S-Corp.

A gradual transition process can help ensure continuity and reduce the risk of disruption when the new leadership takes over.

Documenting the Succession Plan: A well-documented succession plan is critical to avoiding confusion or disputes during a transition.

This plan should outline who will take over key leadership roles, how ownership will be transferred, and any other important details related to the transition.

You may also want to include contingency plans for unexpected events, such as the sudden illness or death of a key owner.

Working with legal and financial advisors will help ensure that the succession plan is comprehensive and legally sound.

Conclusion

Implementing best practices in governance, risk management, and succession planning helps create a resilient and sustainable LLC S-Corp.

By fostering clear communication and decision-making, managing risks effectively, and planning for the future, you can set your business up for long-term success.

In the next chapter, we will wrap up the topics we've covered and explore how to apply all these insights in your day-to-day operations, ensuring that your LLC S-Corp thrives in a competitive business environment.

Conclusion

Chapter 20: Putting it All Together

As we reach the final chapter, it's time to recap the key concepts we've covered and provide you with a clear path forward as an LLC S-Corp owner.

This chapter will summarize the most important lessons, guide you on the next steps, and point you toward resources that can help you continue to grow and improve your business.

Recap of Key Concepts

Throughout this book, we've explored the ins and outs of forming and managing an LLC with S-Corp election.

Here's a quick recap of the key concepts discussed:

Understanding LLCs and S-Corps: We began by defining LLCs and S-Corps, outlining their purpose and key characteristics, and comparing them to other business structures.

LLCs provide flexibility in ownership and management, while S-Corp election offers tax advantages, such as pass-through taxation.

Eligibility and Restrictions: Not everyone can elect S-Corp status. We explored who qualifies, the limitations on ownership, and the need for complaint management structures.

Business Formation Process: We walked through choosing a business name, registering your LLC, obtaining an EIN, and filing articles of organization—all essential steps to legally establish your business.

Operating Agreement: Drafting a solid operating agreement is critical to outlining decision-making processes, ownership rights, and other essential governance elements. We discussed key provisions and provided a sample for reference.

Licenses and Permits: Different industries require different business and professional licenses, as well as local permits. Knowing which ones apply to your business is vital for legal compliance.

Accounting and Taxation: You learned the basics of setting up your accounting and bookkeeping systems, understanding S-Corp taxation (including pass-through taxation), and fulfilling tax filing requirements with forms like 1120S and Schedule K-1.

Tax Strategies and Compliance: We discussed tax strategies to minimize self-employment tax, maximize deductions, and avoid tax pitfalls, while maintaining S-Corp status through compliance with tax laws and annual reporting.

Ownership Changes and Dissolution: We covered the processes for adding or removing owners, changing management, amending the operating agreement, and even dissolving the LLC S-Corp when necessary.

Managing Finances and Employees: Financial management, including budgeting, forecasting, cash flow management, and employee-related issues like recruitment, compensation, and termination, are vital for sustaining growth.

Growth and Risk Management: Best practices for governance, risk management, and succession planning were discussed, ensuring you know how to prepare for long-term success and unexpected changes.

Next Steps for LLC S-Corp Owners

Now that you have a solid understanding of what it takes to form and run an LLC with S-Corp election, it's time to put these lessons into action. Here's what you should do next:

Review Your Current Structure: Whether you're starting from scratch or refining an existing LLC S-Corp, ensure your operating agreement, governance practices, and tax compliance are in order.

Implement Best Practices: From managing finances and taxes to risk management and succession planning, apply the strategies we've discussed to make sure your business is well-positioned for success.

Keep an Eye on Tax Deadlines: Staying compliant with IRS regulations is essential to maintaining your S-Corp status. Ensure you're aware of all tax filing deadlines and requirements, and consider working with a tax professional to avoid costly mistakes.

Plan for Growth: As your business grows, revisit your structure, tax strategies, and governance practices. Growth may require new employees, additional licenses, or a more formalized risk management plan.

Stay Compliant with Laws and Regulations: Make it a habit to review your business licenses, permits, and industry regulations regularly. Compliance ensures that your business can continue operating smoothly without legal interruptions.

Prepare for the Future: If you haven't already, start thinking about succession planning. Whether you plan to pass your business down to a family member or eventually sell it, having a plan in place will make the transition much smoother when the time comes.

Resources for Further Learning

The world of business and taxation is complex, and it's always evolving. To keep up-to-date and continue learning, here are some valuable resources to consider:

IRS Website (irs.gov): The IRS is your primary source of information on federal tax regulations, S-Corp election rules, and tax filing requirements. Their website offers tools and guidance to help you stay compliant.

Small Business Administration (sba.gov): The SBA provides resources for business planning, financing, and management. They also offer information on licensing, legal compliance, and business growth strategies.

LegalZoom (legalzoom.com): If you need help forming your LLC, drafting your operating agreement, or handling other legal tasks, LegalZoom is a popular online legal service for small business owners.

Tax and Business Advisors: Consider working with an accountant, tax advisor, or attorney who specializes in LLCs and S-Corps.

Their expertise can help you optimize your business structure, manage taxes, and navigate legal issues..

Staying informed through continued education will benefit your LLC S-Corp over time.

Conclusion

Forming and managing an LLC S-Corp may seem daunting at first, but by following the steps outlined in this book and applying best practices, you can build a strong foundation for your business. From governance and taxation to risk management and growth strategies, each aspect plays a critical role in ensuring your business thrives.

The journey of running an LLC S-Corp is ongoing, and as your business evolves, so will your responsibilities. By staying informed, adapting to changes, and seeking out resources, you'll be well-equipped to lead your business to long-term success.

www.ingramcontent.com/pod-product-compliance
Lightning Source LLC
Chambersburg PA
CBHW070354230526
45471CB00006B/2569